I Want to Teach
my CHiLD About
Sex

BY

DR. KARL & SHANNON WENDT

Standard

Produced by Susan Lingo Books™
Cover and interior by Diana Walters

12 11 10 09 08 07 06 05   9 8 7 6 5 4 3 2 1
0-7847-1761-3

Contents

Introduction   4

Chapter 1: If You Don't Teach Them, Someone Else Will   8

Most parents are terrified to talk to their kids about sex! 8
Where do most kids learn what they know about sex? 12
God has a plan for learning about sex. 16
Create open communication with your children. 24

Chapter 2: It's Not Too Soon, It's Not Too Late   30

Ages 3–6: Laying the right spiritual foundation. 30
Ages 7–9: Time for The Talk. 40
Ages 10–12: Don't drop the subject now! 44
Ages 13+: It's still not too late. 50
Provide gender-specific information. 54

Chapter 3: Time for The Talk   62

Getting off the ground: How to get started. 62
Bring the message home: God made sex for marriage. ...66
Having sex has consequences. 70

Chapter 4: Use Teachable Moments   74

Use media moments. 74
Use illustrations and object lessons. 78
Use or defuse sex-ed programs in your child's school. 82
Use your personal stories. 86

More Resources 92
Subpoint Index 94

Introduction

*W*hy teach your child about sex?

Our goal in this book is to educate, motivate, and "inspirate" you into the realization that you are the best sex-education teacher your child will ever have. First we will show you why you should take on this task, and then we'll show you how to accomplish it. This book contains four distinct chapters. Chapter 1 will convince you that you are up to this task and will do a great job. The second chapter details the specifics you should cover depending on your individual child's age and gender. The third chapter will prepare you and your child for The Talk, and chapter 4 gives practical and fun ideas for continuing to get the message across through the years.

We are glad that you picked up this book. Talking to your kids about sex will be one of the most important things you will ever do. We pray that this book will make the task easier, more comprehensible, and, ultimately, more doable.

Dr. Karl and Shannon Wendt

Where Do You Stand?

Preparing your child for godly dating, courtship, marriage, and sex is an important part of parenting. The following questionnaire will help you evaluate your own strengths and weaknesses and where your own values and philosophies fit in. Circle the box with the number that best corresponds to your answer. Then add up the total of your answers and check out the How You Scored box! (Retake the quiz after reading the book to see if your score changed!)

OPTIONS

❶ Strongly agree

❷ Agree somewhat

❸ Disagree somewhat

❹ Strongly disagree

I WORK REGULARLY ON MY MARRIAGE, LOOKING FOR MORE UNDERSTANDING AND COMMUNICATION.

❶ ❷ ❸ ❹

I SET ASIDE TIME TO TALK ABOUT LOVE, DATING, AND RELATIONSHIPS WITH MY CHILD.

❶ ❷ ❸ ❹

I AM CAREFUL ABOUT THE SEXUAL CONTENT OF WHAT I VIEW ON TV AND THE INTERNET.

❶ ❷ ❸ ❹

I THINK THAT KIDS TODAY TALK ABOUT SEX AT A YOUNGER AGE THAN WHEN I WAS A CHILD.

❶ ❷ ❸ ❹

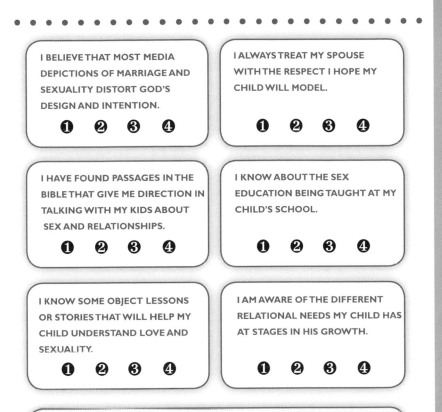

I BELIEVE THAT MOST MEDIA DEPICTIONS OF MARRIAGE AND SEXUALITY DISTORT GOD'S DESIGN AND INTENTION.

❶ ❷ ❸ ❹

I ALWAYS TREAT MY SPOUSE WITH THE RESPECT I HOPE MY CHILD WILL MODEL.

❶ ❷ ❸ ❹

I HAVE FOUND PASSAGES IN THE BIBLE THAT GIVE ME DIRECTION IN TALKING WITH MY KIDS ABOUT SEX AND RELATIONSHIPS.

❶ ❷ ❸ ❹

I KNOW ABOUT THE SEX EDUCATION BEING TAUGHT AT MY CHILD'S SCHOOL.

❶ ❷ ❸ ❹

I KNOW SOME OBJECT LESSONS OR STORIES THAT WILL HELP MY CHILD UNDERSTAND LOVE AND SEXUALITY.

❶ ❷ ❸ ❹

I AM AWARE OF THE DIFFERENT RELATIONAL NEEDS MY CHILD HAS AT STAGES IN HIS GROWTH.

❶ ❷ ❸ ❹

HOW YOU SCORED

10—20 Give yourself a pat on the back! You have a healthy perspective on relationships. You work hard to keep the lines of communication open with your child, even on tough topics. The way you treat others will be reflected in your child and will serve him well throughout his life!

21—31 Your relationships have experienced some ups and some downs. You work to communicate with your child, but sometimes it clicks and sometimes it doesn't. You would love for your child to avoid the mistakes you've experienced.

32—40 You've been hurt a lot and are eager to help your child avoid such pain. You long to be closer to your child but often get frustrated when you make efforts to improve your communication with her. Like all parents, you'd love for your child to have an even better, healthier life. Today is the beginning of that journey ... for your child and for you.

If You Don't Teach Them, Someone Else Will

God has an incredible plan for the way kids should learn about human sexuality, and you are one of the key players. Most kids would rather hear the truth about sex from you than hear half-truths from TV or friends. If we don't teach our kids, someone else will—and we may not like what our kids learn.

Most parents are terrified to talk to their kids about sex!

The birds and the bees. The cabbage patch. The stork. *The Talk.* Parents fear it, kids dread it, and few families have actually discussed it.

We didn't hear it from our parents.

key point
YOU ALREADY HAVE THE LOVE.

Ten years ago we conducted a seminar titled "How to Talk to Your Kids About Sex." We polled that first audience to see how many of them had gotten *The Talk.* Fewer than 10 percent had gotten only a lesson in basic human plumbing. How do we discuss sexuality with our children? What and when should we teach them?

There are ways to make this challenging parental responsibility easier. You don't have to be afraid, and you certainly don't have to be unprepared. But the time will come when you need to be studied-up, prayed-up, and ready to say, "Junior (or Juniorette), it is time we had a little talk."

key point
YOU CAN GAIN THE KNOWLEDGE.

Is there someone saying, "I know people who never got The Talk,

key point
YOU KNOW YOU HAVE THE RESPON-SIBILITY.

and they turned out fine"? Just because someone missed the *big* mistakes doesn't mean he wouldn't have also benefited from parental input. Dialogues about relationships, growth, and development prepare kids for the most important decisions they'll ever make—short of their decision to follow Jesus.

EXCUSES FOR NOT HAVING THE TALK

- "I'm afraid it will plant unhealthy ideas."
- "We live on a farm ... they can figure it out."
- "Some things are best left undiscussed."
- "Shouldn't his father give him the talk?"
- "Shouldn't her mother give her the talk?"
- "My kids won't listen to me..."
- "Oh, we had a little talk ... once ... sorta."

We feel too uncomfortable.

None of us is totally at ease with this topic, so we can't just keep waiting for the magical moment when it "feels right." It is your job as the parent to keep locks on many of those doors until your child is old enough to understand—and some of those doors never need to be opened at all.

key point

MANY PEOPLE FEEL INADEQUATE— BUT YOU CAN DO IT!

key point

IT'S OKAY TO FEEL AWKWARD.

These wonderful children God has put in our charge *will* grow up; they *will* become curious; and they *will* learn about sex from someone. Shouldn't that someone be you? Of course you feel awkward. Of course you feel inadequate. We have five college degrees between us but would rather present The Talk in front of thousands of teens than to discuss sexuality with our own children!

Much of a parent's discomfort in discussing sex comes from his or her own embarrassment. As recent as a generation ago, most religious communities equated discussions of sexuality with being vulgar. But in the right context, sex is a gift from our loving God. How can our children understand the beauty of God's plan if we're too embarrassed to broach the topic?

BETTER THAN NOTHING!

A TV commercial once showed dancing parents using singing sock puppets to talk to their teens about avoiding drug use. The caption read, "Even *this* is better than nothing!" Our message to you: Talk with your kids about sex no matter how "dorky" you feel. It will certainly be better than doing nothing!

TARGET MOMENT

Remember how simple it was to teach your child to blow a kiss? It was probably a bit harder to teach him how to tie his shoes. Teaching your child about sexuality and love is simply another step in guiding him to celebrate the person God has made him to be!

Okay, we agree that we must deal with our children's questions about sex, just as we try to answer questions like, "Are there bathrooms in heaven?" We don't promise that the task is going to be easy. But we will give you enough courage and information to jump-start you and arm you for the job. And today is the best day to begin!

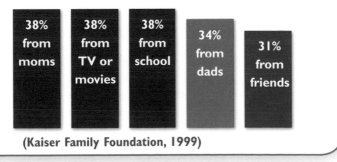

TOP FIVE SOURCES OF SEX EDUCATION ACCORDING TO KIDS 10–12

38% from moms · 38% from TV or movies · 38% from school · 34% from dads · 31% from friends

(Kaiser Family Foundation, 1999)

Where do most kids learn what they know about sex?

Where did you first learn about sex? Most kids learn about sex either from their peers or from the media—and much of what they learn is wrong.

Media: We're not in Mayberry any more!

The media does not care about kids or the child-rearing business. Media's job is to sell products, concepts, and entertainment. We're not saying that you have to throw out the telly, but you must realize that much of what TV and movies teach about sex is wrong and dangerous—and our children will be willing students if we do not intervene.

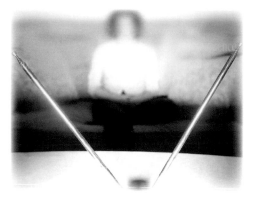

So what do we do? We become informed. For starters, we must realize that prime-time TV viewing is not the safe haven it was when we were kids. And did you know that a movie can receive a PG-13 rating and *still* have female frontal nudity?

MEDIA LIES ABOUT SEX

1. Everyone is doing it—if they're cool and hip, that is.

2. If you're in love, it's okay.

3. There are no consequences to unmarried sexual activity, except, perhaps, becoming more attractive.

4. Do it as soon as you can, as often as you can, with as many people as you can.

5. Married people have boring sex lives.

MOST PARENTS WISH TO LIMIT THEIR CHILDREN'S TV VIEWING.

key point
MEDIA INFLUENCES KIDS.

Our kids tell us they aren't really listening to the words from songs—so how can they sing the lyrics? Don't rely on advisory stickers to be the judge of appropriate lyrics! Check out song words before a purchase is made. Magazines aimed at teens frequently contain question-and-answer columns that can be a conduit for spreading sexually explicit information, much of which is inaccurate.

key point
GUIDE MEDIA CHOICES!

SOLUTION TO THE MEDIA DILEMMA:
Allow your kids to own, play, watch, read, or rent only the entertainment that you've approved. Remember that you are the parent.

Songs, movies, and shows depicting love and human sexuality wouldn't be such a big problem if they were honest teachers. Who (or what) will be your children's human sexuality teacher? Don't hire Hollywood, MTV, or teen magazines to do it ... no matter how hard they try to get the job!

"But, my best friend said... "

"**D**id you learn anything new at school today?" we asked our kindergarten daughter, Sammy. "Well, Billy says that he wants to have sex with Mary," she replied, and we quickly considered selling all our possessions and moving to the hills until she turned thirty-five! But we realized that she needed more information—and sooner than we had anticipated.

key point
TEACH THE TRUTH TO DISPEL MYTHS!

Kids talk about sex more than you think. Ask your elementary-aged son or daughter what his or her friends are saying about sex. You'll be amazed. Ask your junior-high child what his friends say about sex. He'll blush. It is amazing to hear some of the misconceptions that are making the rounds as kids tell other kids what they think are facts.

key point
KIDS ARE GOING TO TALK ABOUT SEX.

SEXUAL MYTHS KIDS HEAR AT SCHOOL

- "**You can't get pregnant the first time you have sex.**"

- "**You can't get pregnant if you *do it* underwater or standing up.**"

- "**You can't get herpes when you're on the pill.**"

- "**My boyfriend couldn't have gotten me pregnant; he doesn't have any armpit hair!**"

✓ **Think back to when you first began learning about your body, sex, and relationships. Ask yourself these important questions as you prepare to help your child travel the same road to adulthood!**

- *What did your parents tell you about sex? At what age?*
- *What did they say that was helpful? What was not helpful?*
- *What ideas did you have that were mistaken?*
- *What do you want to do differently?*

Every day that you put off talking to your kids about sex, the likelihood for misinformation increases. We teach our children about Jesus at an early age in order to firmly fix in their minds fundamental spiritual truths. Similarly, we must bring up the topic of sex and give our children correct, God-based information before they are confronted with and confused by the half-truths they hear.

My (Karl's) first memory of hearing the word *sex* was with a couple of next-door neighbor boys when I was eight. They showed me magazines with pictures of naked women and explained the reproductive process. Had they known, my wonderful Christian parents would have been appalled. The point is this: Kids are going to talk. Whether or not they know what they are talking about matters little. We must beat their peers to the punch.

Kids learn both good and bad information from one another. Which of these do you want your eight-year-old to learn from another eight-year-old?

- *Where a baby comes from and how it got there.*
- *Names for body parts.*
- *What happens on honeymoons.*

God has a plan for learning about sex.

This may surprise you, but God has a plan for the way He wants our kids to learn about sex, and He is not silent on this issue in His Word. His plan is wonderful and beautiful.

The Bible addresses the issue of teaching kids about sex.

key point
GOD HAS A DESIGN FOR SEX WITHIN MARRIAGE.

key point
GOD'S TRUTH TEACHES US.

Do you remember the classic Bill Cosby comedy routine about Noah? Cosby's voice for God reassuringly told Noah about the upcoming flood and that he must build an ark. Noah queried, "Riiiight … what's an ark?" Noah just didn't get it … until the Lord boomed, "Noah!!!! How long can you tread water?"

Even the God in Cosby's hilarious version of the story gave specific instructions in clear, understandable language. He patiently answered Noah's questions. That's God's nature—and He wants us to do the same with our children: to clearly communicate His will regarding sex to them in clear, understandable language and to answer the questions they will inevitably have.

Studying the Bible provides truth and teaching—even about sex, love, and relationships.

Ten Commandments
(Exodus 20:3-17)

1. You shall have no other gods before me.
2. You shall not make for yourself an idol.
3. You shall not misuse the name of the LORD your God.
4. Remember the Sabbath day by keeping it holy.
5. Honor your father and your mother.
6. You shall not murder.
7. **You shall not commit adultery.**
8. You shall not steal.
9. You shall not give false testimony against your neighbor.
10. **You shall not covet your neighbor's house [or] wife.**

The Ten Commandments provide a great plan for a well-lived life, but can they help teach about sex? Look at commandments seven and ten. They deal directly with issues of sexual behavior and make no sense without a basic concept of God's design for sex within marriage. Teaching our kids to obey these two commandments without teaching them something about sex is like instructing someone to build an ark in cubits … and never telling him what those words mean!

We wouldn't instruct our kids not to steal without providing a basic knowledge of what it means to own something. We wouldn't teach them not to have idols while refusing to explain what an idol is. A commandment means something only if we understand what we're being asked to do or to avoid. Both commandments seven and ten make it clear that purity matters to God. To properly communicate the message of these commandments to our children, we must be willing to bring up the subject of sex.

By age thirteen, friends take over as the number one influence in kids' lives and Dad drops off the chart! Teach your kids while you can!

These "talks" are our responsibility—both Mom's and Dad's.

"Yes," we hear someone saying, "I see how important it is for kids to learn about sex from a mature, God-fearing adult. *But why does it have to be me?* I don't know what to say. Hey, could Karl or Shannon take my kid and give him The Talk?" Well, as much as we would like to, God has given this awesome responsibility to *you!*

key point
KIDS NEED TO LEARN FROM MOM AND DAD.

"LISTEN, MY SON, TO YOUR FATHER'S INSTRUCTION AND DO NOT FORSAKE YOUR MOTHER'S TEACHING."

(Proverbs 1:8)

DAUGHTERS NEED DADS TO:

- tell them how beautiful they are.
- explain how boys think.
- love, hug, and listen to them.
- show them a real gentleman.

We've also heard, "Hey, we've only got daughters—that's their mom's responsibility, isn't it?" Or, "We've been blessed with boys. I guess this talk thing falls on Dad, right?" Wrong! Proverbs 1:8 is clear in involving *both* parents. Not to fear, single parents, you can get the job done—and do it well, too!

SONS NEED MOMS TO:

- tell them how strong they are.
- explain how girls feel.
- love, hug, and listen to them.
- teach them to honor women.

"**O**ur school has an excellent sex-education program. Isn't that enough?" There certainly are good programs out there, but there are also some really bad ones—and even the best school-based program is missing something every kid needs (and actually wants): parents. Even Christian schools that include spiritual principles in the classroom can't replace the power of a *father's instruction and a mother's teaching.*

PARENTS POINTER

Take equal responsibility! Proverbs 1:8 mentions both "your father's instruction" and "your mother's teaching." Sounds like the writer meant both Mom and Dad, doesn't it? Remember to share in educating your child as God desires!

"**W**hat about the church? We have a great youth program. I guess that lets me off the hook." Sorry. Not even an awesome youth minister can take your place in communicating God's plan for love and sex in marriage. By the time your kids are in youth group, they've probably gathered flawed information. No one knows, loves, or understands your kids like you. Like it or not, no one can do the job better, or has more invested in the results,

key point

YOUR CHILD IS COUNTING ON YOU!

"Our children are not going to be just 'our children'— they are going to be other people's husbands and wives and the parents of our grandchildren."
—Mary S. Calderone

These are always ongoing chats and talks.

Wouldn't it be nice if we could tell our children something just once and be assured that they would "get it," and we would never have to bring up the subject again? Continued parental involvement is essential for the academic growth and progress of our children. So why do some parents feel they can adequately cover all they need to teach their children about sex in a one-time talk?

key point
EDUCATING KIDS IS AN ONGOING PROCESS.

Read aloud Deuteronomy 6:6-9, then as parents ask your-selves the following questions:

- *When is the best time to talk to my child?*

- *How can I use different times during the day or evening to approach my child in talking about life, sex, and relationships?*

- *Why is it important to tie my teachings to God's truths and His plans?*

- *What can I do today to improve communication with my child?*

We stay very involved in the academic lives of our children. Is school more important than relationships? Are academic decisions more important than sexual decisions? Our input is vital in both areas!

Obviously, instructing our children in the ways of the Lord is not a one-time task. We are to look for opportunities to discuss God's purposes from the moment we gently awaken our kids in the morning to the time we tuck them into bed at night—in other words, all throughout the day. This directive is particularly important as it applies to teaching your children about their sexuality.

It would be so much simpler if we could just hand our kids a book, give them a little kiss, and wish them well. But that's not how it works. Even very young children will have little questions that need to be addressed thoughtfully and not pushed aside until the "big talk" when your child reaches the age of seven to nine.

Things we wish we had to do only once . . .

Tell our kids to eat their vegetables.

Pay taxes.

Gas up the car.

Clean house.

Talk to our kids about SEX!

TARGET MOMENT

The "big talk" should be neither the first nor the last conversation you have with your child about sex. Learning about love and relationships is an ongoing process!

Often our best opportunities to share God's plan for sexuality with our children will involve watching for "teachable moments" and using them well. In many ways these ongoing, when-you-sit-at-home, when-you-walk-along-the-road, when-you-lie-down, and when-you-get-up moments can be the most important opportunities of all for communicating with your child!

These talks should be positive.

A few years ago we were asked to speak at a convention of youth ministers on enhancing sexual relations in marriage. We titled our presentation "Sex Is Not a Four-Letter Word." Ministers loved the title—and the presentation. Our message was that even ministers and their wives have every right to a wonderful, healthy, fulfilling sex life. The Bible is surprisingly and refreshingly frank and straightforward on this issue.

key point
GOD'S PLAN FOR MARRIAGE IS BEAUTIFUL.

God's commandment to the first man and woman was to populate the earth, to procreate, to have sex. Sex is God's beautiful idea, but throughout history cultures have vacillated from glorifying sex to treating it as disgraceful. Both extremes are misguided. Of course, it is true that sex outside of marriage carries enormous negative spiritual, emotional, and physical consequences. But that does not lessen the fact that God purposefully made the sexual experience to be an enjoyable, natural, and beautiful means of expressing love between a husband and wife.

Regardless of our own past and personal struggles, we must make certain never to let our tone, demeanor, or words suggest to our children that sex is dirty, wrong or unpleasant.

Though some people view God's commands as divine attempts to deny them pleasure, rightly understood and obeyed, God's Word enhances our lives. We must make it a priority to present God's plan for sex to our children as a beautiful gift from a loving God—*a garland to grace their heads, a chain to adorn their necks.*

key point
GOD'S PLAN FOR SEX IS GOOD.

Read aloud Genesis 1:28 and Ecclesiastes 3:1 with your child. Then discuss the following questions:

• *Why do you think God created people to have families?*

• *How are parents, babies, and children part of God's plan for the world?*

• *Why is it good that God is in control and has plans for His people?*

As a professional counselor, I (Karl) frequently encounter individuals who have experienced traumatic sexual abuse. Of course, it is especially difficult for these individuals to describe sex positively to their children. Others have been told that sex is wrong for so many years that they continue to feel guilty about sex even after marriage. If you are struggling with misconceptions about sex, please get help for yourself before you pass any crippling beliefs on to your kids.

DON'T FORGET

Help your child realize that, in the context of a loving and respectful marriage, sex is wonderful, fulfilling, and godly.

Create open communication with your children.

If there ever was a time to use the stuff you learned in your speech communication class, this is it! Can't find your notes? Have no fear. This is not really about making a speech. In fact, the best way to get started is simply to listen.

Give focused attention with time and listening.

In his books, Dr. Gary Chapman has described five "love languages" that express love, affection, and attention: words of affirmation, gifts, acts of service, physical touch, and quality time. Kids need generous portions of all five, but when asked which they want most, kids almost always pick quality *time*.

key point

WE EARN THE RIGHT TO TALK BY LISTENING.

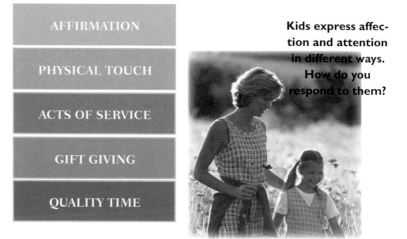

| AFFIRMATION |
| PHYSICAL TOUCH |
| ACTS OF SERVICE |
| GIFT GIVING |
| QUALITY TIME |

Kids express affection and attention in different ways. How do you respond to them?

Just because we are physically with our children does not necessarily mean that they are experiencing the benefit of our full attention. If we hope to share our values with our children and plant in them a conviction to make the best possible sexual choices, we must be willing to listen to them. We earn the right to talk by listening.

It's often said that God gave everyone two ears and only one mouth for a reason. I (Karl) took an entire college-level class in listening. We studied listening and read books on listening—and guess what we did for homework? We listened. I cemented some of my best friendships during that semester. Why? Because I really listened.

Young kids love to talk. We recall young Katie waking up in the morning and wanting to tell us about her dreams in incredible detail. Tune in to your kids. Sure, the opportunities will sometimes come at awkward moments, but grab as many as you can. Inconvenient or not, you'll be glad you did. And by listening, you'll earn the privilege of having your kids listen to you.

LESS-IMPORTANT PLACES OUR MINDS GO WHEN WE HALF-WAY LISTEN TO OUR KIDS

BACK TO WORK
(Why do we want to go back *there?*)

TO MISTAKES WE'VE MADE
(Why re-live those?)

TO ALL THE THINGS WE HAVE LEFT TO DO
(Why think of that *now?*)

Realize that everything you do communicates to your child.

It had been a rough week. Dad tried to put a "good face" on it all. Even so, it was obvious that he was stressed. "What's wrong, Daddy?" said a little voice. Dad paused and looked down at his four-year-old daughter. "Nothing, sweetheart. Everything's fine," he said. The little girl just stared back at her hero. "Daddy, your mouth says everything's fine, but your face says something else."

key point
KIDS READ OUR NONVERBAL SIGNALS.

Sometimes it's hard to remember that how we say something matters as much as what we say. And our kids can often pick up on the feelings we think are hidden behind our words. The tone of our voice, the look on our face, and the gestures we make account for much of our communication. Let's be honest. Talking about sex makes us feel uncomfortable, so we must be especially careful not to unintentionally let our words say "beauty of God's design" while our nonverbal signals scream out "dirty, wrong, and embarrassing."

TARGET MOMENT

When we talk to our kids about sex, we want our words and our nonverbal communication to express the beauty of God's plan for love, children, sex, and relationships.

Researchers say that over 90 percent of a message is communicated through **nonverbal** means.

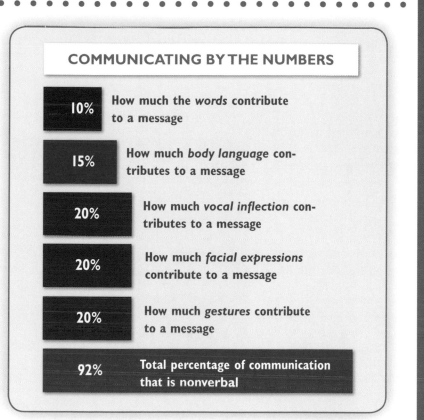

COMMUNICATING BY THE NUMBERS

10%	How much the *words* contribute to a message
15%	How much *body language* contributes to a message
20%	How much *vocal inflection* contributes to a message
20%	How much *facial expressions* contribute to a message
20%	How much *gestures* contribute to a message
92%	Total percentage of communication that is nonverbal

Eye contact is a vital communication tool that speaks volumes to our kids. Depending on his age, it can actually help to be *doing* something with your child that minimizes the need for eye contact. Taking a walk, riding in the car, or even working on a model train can help dispel some of the awkwardness we may feel in talking about sex.

key point
WE MUST COMMUNICATE CAREFULLY.

Here's a brain teaser. You cannot *not* communicate. Everything we do or don't do, say or don't say sends messages that are being interpreted by our kids. Let's make those messages intentional. Let's make the messages *behind* our words be ones of love, security, respect, and confidence as we teach our kids about sex.

Make it fun—if you can.

"*Just a spoonful of sugar helps the medicine go down....*" Remember that song from the classic Disney movie *Mary Poppins*? We've all experienced the frustration of trying to get our kids to do their chores or other tiresome tasks. Rather than lecture or raise her voice, Ms. Poppins's creative solution was to take the boring tasks and give them life, to make them fun.

> "With every job that must be done, there is an element of fun. You find the fun and snap—the job's a game!"
>
> —Mary Poppins

So how do we make talking about sex fun? Kids love stories. Kids love object lessons. Kids love games. We should use each liberally in teaching all of life's lessons to our little ones—especially lessons about sex. I (Shannon) run an abstinence-only sex-education program called Virtuous Reality that instructs over eight thousand sixth- to ninth-grade students in Missouri, Oklahoma, and Kansas each year. My staff and I conduct frequent training sessions to prepare the more than forty presenters we send into classrooms. Guess what we try to impress upon them? Make it fun! Use visual aids. Yes, know your topic: learn the facts, have the heart, and speak the truth. But kids will still tune you out unless you keep them engaged.

key point

KIDS TUNE IN TO FUN.

Children love to learn but hate to be taught, so a wise parent makes learning memorable and fun!

One illustration students enjoy is "The Rose." A presenter passes a rose around the classroom as she describes its beauty and frailty. Each person is allowed to smell and touch the petals—or take a petal to keep. By the time the rose makes the rounds, there are usually no petals left, and all the leaves are gone. Then a new, untouched, unblemished rose is held up next to the one that has made the rounds. The point is clear. One was used, one was protected. One was treated casually, one was cherished. We ask, "If on your wedding day you actually gave a rose to your future mate that symbolized your sexual purity, which one would you want to present or receive?"

> **"I HEAR AND I FORGET,**
> **I SEE AND I REMEMBER,**
> **I DO AND I UNDERSTAND."**
> **—ancient proverb**

"The Rose" (and other visual aids) works on multiple levels. Yes, it grabs their attention. But perhaps just as important is its value as an ongoing communication shortcut. Years after using such an illustration, just a few words can quickly resurrect the message and its impact. These "spoons full of sugar" you use along the way will not only help "the medicine go down" but will also maximize the medicine's positive effect and help ensure that your kids keep listening through the years to come.

TIPS FOR 'TWEENS

Ask your kids to name couples they know who care for each other. Now ask them to tell how you know whether or not a couple really loves each other. This can be a great way to open discussions about family, love, and commitment.

It's Not Too Soon;
It's Not Too Late

Okay, so you're convinced that you need to talk with your kids about sex. But at what age? And what do you say? This chapter is a practical guide that spells out what you need to discuss with your children at various stages in their development.

Ages 3–6: Laying the Right Spiritual Foundation

It is during the formative years that we must lay a spiritual foundation for our children's deepening understanding of the body God has blessed them with and God's design for families.

God made your body and said, "It is good!"

Three- to six-year-olds are discovering their bodies and what those bodies can do. Kids who feel good about who they are and how they look are less likely to grow up with a hunger for physical affirmation that can lead to early, inappropriate sexual activity.

TIPS FOR BUILDING SELF-ESTEEM

- Avoid false praise; give honest compliments.
- Be wary of comparative (smarter, faster, stronger) praise.
- Praise effort more than achievement.
- Tell your kids they look "just right."
- Avoid criticizing others' bodies.
- Avoid constantly criticizing your own body.

key point
GOD MADE US "VERY GOOD."

Here's a great idea for planting a little of that positive body image in your kids. Your three- to six-year-old has probably learned the story of creation in Sunday school class. The story has wonderful application here. At the end of each of the first five days of creation, God paused to reflect on what He had made, and on each day He saw that "it was good." On the sixth day, He created man and woman and said that special creation "was very good!" Tell your kids that God made their bodies and is very proud of His work!

key point
KIDS DESERVE TO FEEL GREAT ABOUT THEIR BODIES.

We are indeed "fearfully and wonderfully made." Teach your child that God made us as we are—the perfect and imperfect parts, the public and the private parts, the whole thing—and our bodies are good. This leads us to the next three building blocks in our sex-education foundation: privacy, modesty, and respect.

Boys and girls are different.

What are the first words uttered after the delivery of a new baby? "It's a boy!" or "You're the proud parents of a sweet baby girl!" Gender matters—to parents and, at a very early age, to kids. Awareness of gender difference is one of a child's first discoveries as he develops an understanding of personal identity. It is from you that your child first learns the meaning of the terms *boy* and *girl* or *mom* and *dad*. It is extremely important for parents to frankly and honestly teach kids at a very young age the physical differences between boys and girls.

key point
GENDER DIFFERENCES ARE IMPORTANT TO KIDS.

key point
THINK ABOUT USING CORRECT TERMINOLOGY.

Think about using correct terminology. Slang words, often used because of our discomfort with explicit sexual terms, just promote confusion and usually end up being more crude than their accurate counterparts. Terms such as *wee-wee* or *pee-pee* are less desirable than simply telling kids that boys have penises and girls have vaginas. The following two stories are perfect examples of the danger of using euphemisms.

Find someone with a litter of puppies or kittens. This is a great time to talk about all babies needing a mommy and a daddy. It will be a great family outing to see the new arrivals—and not end up with a new pet!

A secretary who worked for us had three small boys who called their penises "tweeters." All was well until a new stereo was installed in their car. The mechanic told them he installed a CD player in the dash, a subwoofer in the trunk, and tweeters in the doors. The kids froze. As they drove off, one of the kids whispered, "Mom—there's tweeters ... in the doors!"

IDENTITY DEVELOPMENT BEGINS WITH GENDER AWARENESS.

PARENTS POINTER

Ask your young child to tell you the differences he or she has noticed between boys and girls. You may hear funny answers involving sugar and spice or puppy-dog tails, but your little boy needs to know that girls have a vagina, and your little girl needs to know that boys have a penis.

We were playing cards with some friends when their young boys suddenly seemed too quiet. We peeked to see their sons looking through an old high-school yearbook. The older boy whispered and pointed at faces saying, "Penis ... no penis...." Although we do recommend using correct terminology, we also think it wise to help kids develop an understanding of the right time and place to discuss sexual information.

Privacy, modesty, and respect all matter!

Cute little three-year-old Daniel was visiting his dad at the office when he suddenly had to use the restroom. As he was sitting on the stool, he noticed two work boots in the stall next to him. (They were attached to a repairman on his break.) Moments later, the repairman joined us all in the office. Daniel stared at his boots, then at his face, then loudly asked, "Are *you* the guy who was in there poopin' when I was in there poopin'?" Unabashed, the roofer smiled and said, "Yep, and I sure feel better. How 'bout you?"

TARGET MOMENT

Practice makes perfect—or at least it helps! Have your child name things that are fine to talk about in public, then things that aren't to be talked about aloud in public. After a bit of practice, your child will recognize what's acceptable and what isn't.

It is our task to teach our kids the concepts of privacy, modesty, appropriateness, and respect. The key is to be clear, firm, and unruffled. Parents often over-react, but agitation sends the wrong message. We don't want our kids to think that any parts of their bodies are wrong. We *do* want them to learn the right time, place, and way to discuss such matters.

Teach your child modesty by modeling it yourself.

DON'T FORGET

Kids don't have many "filters," and many terrified parents have returned home from an outing, white-faced, complaining to their spouses, "You'll never believe what *your* child just said!" Be patient—you're not alone!

This is the perfect age to let kids know that certain parts of their bodies are special and should stay covered by clothing. If your son shows his new "undies," let him know that underwear is something special and private, but don't make him feel dirty or nasty. Fear and disgust are contagious. We must gently teach our children privacy and modesty without unintentionally planting negative messages about sexuality.

key point
KNOW HOW TO KEEP PRIVATE THINGS PRIVATE.

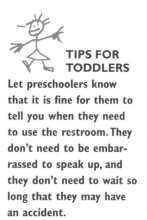

TIPS FOR TODDLERS

Let preschoolers know that it is fine for them to tell you when they need to use the restroom. They don't need to be embarrassed to speak up, and they don't need to wait so long that they may have an accident.

Children need to know that their private body parts are so special that no one else may touch them. You will, of course, establish healthy exceptions for caregivers, but make it clear what is allowable for even those few. Tell your children that if anyone touches them inappropriately, they must tell Mom or Dad right away. The likelihood of abuse is significantly reduced when children receive a simple, calm description of what kind of touching is appropriate.

key point
KEEP COM- MUNICATION OPEN!

God wants kids to be raised by loving families.

It was early on a Saturday morning, and the kids wanted to watch cartoons with me. Right after the cartoon scoundrel did something particularly villainous, my older daughter, Katie, said, "Where is his mommy?" "I don't know, sweetheart," I yawned. "Maybe he doesn't have one." "What?" she cried indignantly. "Of course he has a mommy! And right now I really think his mommy needs to give him a timeout!"

key point
GOD HAS A PLAN FOR FAMILIES.

You'll discover much of what kids have already learned about family roles by watching them play. When your daughter pretends to be a mommy, is she gentle? If your son plays a daddy, does he prop his feet up and demand that everyone be quiet and bring him his dinner? It is always amusing (and quite often humbling) to see your own words and actions reflected in the behavior of your child.

Since we live in a culture that has little respect for God's design for roles within the home, it is even more important that our teaching be intentional. We must purposefully teach our children both verbally and through example about God's plan for families.

key point
MODEL BEING A GODLY FAMILY.

So what do we want our kids to learn about families? Many of the basics are simple yet profound. Children are to "obey [their] parents in the Lord." Dad is the ultimate spiritual leader of the home, commissioned by God with the responsibility of bringing up children in the "training and instruction of the Lord" (Ephesians 6:1, 4). Mom is his

key point
CHILDREN ARE TO OBEY THEIR PARENTS.

partner, and together they make decisions for the good of the family. God wants a husband to love his wife and care so deeply about her needs that he is willing to make great sacrifices. God wants a wife to respect her husband and help him feel like the leader God means for him to be.

Show your kids what it means to be a godly dad. Show them what it means to be a godly mom. These lessons are better modeled than spoken. Like it or not, you are the patterns that will shape their concepts of mom, of dad, and of family.

MUCH OF WHAT WE TEACH IS UNINTENTIONAL AND COMMUNICATED BY OUR ACTIONS.

Read aloud Ephesians 6:1-4 with your child, then discuss the following questions about families:

• *What can children learn from these verses?*

• *What can moms and dads learn from these verses?*

• *Why does God want families to work together?*

• *How can we show our family members we love them?*

Little questions deserve little answers.

Little Johnny came home from kindergarten one day and said, "Mommy, where did I come from?" She had been dreading the question for years. She gulped hard, took a deep breath, and dived in. And she really did a rather impressive job describing the fertilization of the egg, the fallopian tubes, the birth canal. Finally, an hour later, exhausted and more than a little proud of herself, she said to little Johnny, "Well, what do you think?" To which the boy replied, "Okay, but I still don't know where I came from. Jacob in my class is from Cleveland. What about me? Where did I come from?"

TIPS FOR TODDLERS

Be prepared when your toddler and preschool child asks tough questions such as these:

- Will I see Rover in Heaven?
- Where does fire go when it is out?
- What is sex?
- Did Sissy's penis fall off?
- Why can't I use my pretty ruffled panties for Show-n-Tell?

Little questions deserve little answers, and for three- to six-year-olds, the odds are good your little answers will suffice for now. But with some foresight, many not-so-little questions can be anticipated, giving us time to prepare our not-more-than-necessary answers. A frequent question is: "How does a baby get in a mommy's tummy?" A simple answer about God helping the mom and dad plant the baby there will usually satisfy your younger child's inquiring mind.

A poster we once read said: "The average four-year-old asks 437 questions per day." I don't know about the research, but the number is probably not far off. Kids love to ask questions. All the time, over and over— whether or not they even want answers. Often questions just mean, "Listen to me. Talk to me. Pay attention to me."

key point
USE SIMPLE ANSWERS FOR YOUNGER KIDS.

key point
DON'T OFFER MORE THAN KIDS CAN HANDLE.

Young children don't always make the connections we think they do. A child who knows that babies grow in a mommy's tummy may not even think to ask how they get there in the first place.

Even when kids do want an answer, they don't want a lecture. A straightforward question like "What is sex?" warrants a simple response. "Sex is something wonderful God made for moms and dads. Hey, want to play some catch?" Use honesty and simplicity, use a little directness (as much as your child can handle), and try a little redirection. Remember, you are laying a foundation. The Talk is just around the corner.

Ages 7–9: Time for The Talk

All indications are that it is time for *The Talk*. If you have been talking with your child, the foundation has already been laid. Just ease on down the road. Now is the time to do whatever it takes to get you and your child ready.

Heighten their curiosity and anticipation.

Movie previews are designed to generate excitement for the film and pique your interest while it leaves you wanting more. Use this same principle in "previewing" The Talk. You don't need to tell much of the story. Certainly don't give away the big plot twist at the end. But let your child know that a special talk is on the way.

TO MAKE THE TALK REALLY SPECIAL, LET YOUR CHILD HELP IN THE PLANNING.

There are many ways to orchestrate this event, and the decision needs to be based on what will work best with your child. For example, you could go to your child's favorite restaurant, even if fast-food burgers are still his idea of "fine dining." You can build anticipation by telling her that this is an event that has been planned for a long time. It could be a camping trip, an overnight stay at a fun hotel, or a special-day outing. The point is to schedule a specific time and find a place that will be free from interruptions.

If this is your first child, then the whole event will be new and possibly confusing. Some experts suggest that you tell your child that she is now old enough to hear the "fantastic secret." Now, I don't think the "fantastic secret" angle would have worked well with our kids—they wouldn't think it was too fantastic, and at that age they probably would have wanted it to remain a secret. But the special-event idea is likely to be a winner. It will be easier with your subsequent children. Having been informed by their older siblings, they will begin to anticipate their turn. As the birthdays march on, they will know that their own special outing is coming.

key point

NOW IS THE TIME TO GET READY.

Okay, so you have heightened your child's curiosity—have you heightened your blood pressure, too? You want to know if you can take an outline, note cards, or crib sheets. You'd better! If you have really thought through and planned out how this event is going to unfold, you are going to need your notes. Hey, the kids will think it's funny.

TARGET MOMENT

So, how do you begin? You might start by remembering questions you had as a child.

• Where did you go to get answers?
• Who did you ask?
• Did you just guess?
• How did you feel after the big talk?

key point

MAKE THIS A SPECIAL TIME!

Make your child feel "grown up."

Our Aunt Julia told us about a friend who was having The Talk with his nine-year-old son. The dad thought all was fine until the boy burst into sobs and whimpered, "Do I *have* to do *that?*" We assume his attitude will change in time for his wedding, but for now his response is not uncommon. Even if you never say "and that is what we did to make you," your child will figure that out on his own.

Your children need to feel they have earned the right to this new level of knowledge. We do not want to burden our children with information they are not ready for. If your children believe that you believe they are ready for The Talk, then they are much more likely to be able to handle the information.

> *"Everything is boring if you lecture—even sex, so listen rather than lecture your kids. Have a conversation. Don't fill in the blanks. Find out what they want to know, and don't feel the need to give them more or less."*
>
> **—Sociologist Pepper Schwartz**

Our culture has few rites of passage for our pubescent children, so they frequently create their own. Our sons cannot kill the mighty buffalo, nor can our daughters use ceremonial piercing and tattooing to show that they are now women—although some try. We have a few accepted signs of maturity, but our kids need more. Use The Talk as a great chance to show them they are now of age. You are presenting them with their first hunting spear; you are letting them know the village secrets. Be proud of your children as they cross over into the first stages of adulthood, and be proud of yourself that you have raised them well.

Our goal as parents is to nurture our children in our family values, pace their social growth, and launch them into the world. It takes a light touch and good timing. We don't want to push them too fast, and we certainly don't want to retard their independence and self-confidence. The Talk is an excellent opportunity for you to show your children that you really believe in them.

Help your kids feel more mature by giving them new "rites of passage."

- **Agree on a later bedtime or curfew.**
- **Let them decorate their rooms in their own way.**
- **Let them do their own laundry (it will be fun for a while).**
- **Give them more voting power on entertainment choices.**
- **Tell them that they are maturing and doing well.**
- **Give them a chance to stretch their wings with small jobs,**

key point

MAKE YOUR CHILD FEEL SPECIAL.

Ages 10–12: Don't drop the subject now!

Whew! You made it through The Talk! And to your surprise, neither you nor your child ran out of the room screaming with your hands covering your ears. But don't put down this book yet! There is much more your child needs to know, and it needs to come from you.

Puberty, growth, and change do happen!

This developmental stage (ten to twelve) is the perfect time to follow up The Talk with important information that goes beyond the "plumbing." By the time children enter their teen years, they typically exhibit some degree of rebellion, cynicism, or skepticism, but *'tweenagers* are still optimistic and conversational. Use this time to prepare your child for the many changes and challenges that lie directly ahead.

Do you remember going through adolescence? We sure do! And nothing in the world could convince us to experience all the pimples, raging hormones, body hair and odor, growth spurts, and mood swings again! Now is a time that our children need extra reassurance, encouragement, and knowledge of the transitions that are to come.

TIPS FOR 'TWEENS

In order to provide reassurance, encouragement, and the knowledge of the changes to come, be sure to keep the lines of communication open and direct with your 'tween!

When is the last time you considered moving into a different home or launching into a new job? Change is often accompanied by anxiety and unease. But accurate information and thorough preparation help us make informed decisions, and wise choices—and can set our hearts at rest in anxious times.

CONSIDER THIS ...
Some things are less stressful with advance warning:

DINNER GUESTS

JOB CHANGES

SUDDEN GROWTH OF BODY HAIR IN STRANGE PLACES

THE BEGINNING OF THE MENSTRUAL CYCLE

MAJOR EXAMS IN SCHOOL

ERECTIONS AND WET DREAMS

ZITS AND OTHER COMPLEXION PROBLEMS

HORMONE-INDUCED MOOD FLUCTUATIONS

FINANCIAL AUDITS

Kids ten to twelve are in the *transition stage*. Girls need to be prepared for the growth of their breasts, pubic hair, and menstrual cycles. Boys need advance warning about voice changes, erections, and wet dreams. Both genders need preparation for changes in complexion, slight pains from rapid body growth, and hormone-induced mood fluctuations.

Be forewarned and forearmed!

When is the best time to prepare for a really big project or test? We usually perform better on challenging projects when we plan far in advance, create a reasonable strategy for completion, and even anticipate the most likely distractions that could thwart our goals. When we plan in advance, our heads are clearer, our thinking is better, and we are usually much more proud of the results.

TARGET MOMENT

Things not to put off until the very last second:

• cracking a book to study for a test
• deciding what to do in case of a fire
• learning which string opens your parachute
• knowing how to refuse unwanted sexual advances
• knowing how to deal with sexual urges

key point

HELP KIDS BE READY FOR CHANGES.

When is the best time to decide how far to go on a date? When should you begin creating a mental picture of the kind of person you would like to marry? The answers are obvious: before you are in the middle of an awkward situation. When the outcome really matters, it makes sense not to wait until the final moment.

Consider the importance of emergency preparedness. No school administrator would wait for a fire before determining the safest, wisest course of action in such an emergency. These decisions are so important we even *practice* carrying out emergency plans. When our children's lives are on the line, we do not want a last-minute, poorly designed, fly-by-the-seat-of-your-pants strategy. There is simply too much at stake.

key point
USE "SEXUAL PREPARED-NESS."

My (Shannon) staff teaches students how to prepare for dating, love, sex, and marriage. Many times students have told us that they have used the actual tools and words we practiced in class. "Sexual preparedness" involves deciding in advance how far to go on a date and what kind of movies are worth watching. A fire drill may save our kids' lives. A refusal skill may save their hearts.

PREPARING YOUR KIDS FOR CHANGING BODIES AND EMOTIONS CAN LESSEN THEIR FEAR OF THE UNKNOWN.

WHAT DO 10- TO 12-YEAR-OLDS WORRY ABOUT MOST?

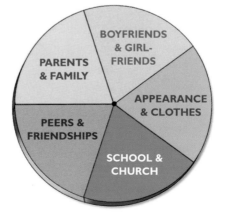

BOYFRIENDS & GIRL-FRIENDS

PARENTS & FAMILY

APPEARANCE & CLOTHES

PEERS & FRIENDSHIPS

SCHOOL & CHURCH

Don't avoid the tough topics.

We occasionally hear a parent say, "But my kid is only ten, eleven, twelve! And you want me to talk to him about topics like homosexuality and masturbation? You've got to be kidding!" We're not kidding. And you may as well add to the list other such doozies as abortion, prostitution, rape, sexual abuse, and birth control. Your preteen child will soon learn all about the tough topics. Don't you think he deserves to hear the truth from you?

key point
YOUR KIDS DESERVE TO HEAR THE TRUTH ... FROM YOU.

Simple definitions and reasonably poker-faced explanations—these are what kids need most when learning about tough sexual subjects. Seize this early opportunity to inoculate your child against the confused values of our world by providing even-keeled explanations of each difficult topic. Many good resources go deeper into these issues, but if you do consult other resources, consider utilizing the following simple litmus test.

key point
BE BRAVE! TACKLE TOUGH TOPICS.

PARENTS POINTER

Instead of changing the subject, as many parents do, take advantage of opportunities to discuss tough issues to clear up any questions or confusion and to impart your own values.

To find if a book is in line with your values, locate the paragraphs devoted to both homosexuality and birth control. Read those sections first. If you agree with what the book says, we virtually guarantee that you will concur with the rest of the work. This world has a wisdom of its own, but we have been made *by* and *for* God, so He knows how we work and what we need. His ways are not only right; they are best.

> **Search your Bible and your heart before you share your own educated values with your children.**

I (Karl) will never forget being in seventh grade and visiting a good friend. The whole family was watching the news when a reporter broke a story

about a prostitution ring. Unfamiliar with the concept, I innocently asked, "What's a prostitution ring?" The room froze. Time stood still. Finally, the father of the family smiled and said, "Why don't you ask your parents?" Good advice.

Explain the issues of homosexuality, rape, sexual abuse, prostitution, and abortion—and let your child know that these are all mentioned in the Bible as being outside of God's plan. Discuss the more complicated issues of masturbation and birth control. Neither topic is dealt with directly in Scripture, and Christian experts have varying opinions on each. Know where (and why) you stand on these issues and share that with your kids.

What are tough topics kids face? Help your kids know where you and your faith stand on each.

- Homosexuality
- Rape
- Sexual Abuse
- Prostitution
- Masturbation
- Abortion
- Birth Control

Ages 13+: It's still not too late.

This age involves topics such as contraceptives and parties, and your child will be caught in the classic struggle of what and who to believe. You must be a warrior in this battle.

Debunking the lies.

It is easier to fight the lies if you are aware of the lies. Pick up copies of teen magazines to catch up on the buzz. Check the history on your computer to see what sites have been visited and watch some of your kid's favorite TV shows. Discover some of the lies your children are being exposed to.

A few years ago I (Shannon) was teaching a class of eighth-graders about sex and dating when a girl asked, "So, are you saying that I don't have to have sex in ninth grade? My girlfriends and I were talking about when we start dating in ninth grade and how everyone has sex on the second or third date, and we just aren't too excited about that." I told her that her body and her choices were hers alone to control. I told her that many people do not have sex before they are married, and many people don't even date in high school at all. I watched her skip down the hall like the child that she was. She stopped, turned, and said to me, "You know what, Mrs. Wendt? Ninth grade might not be so bad after all."

key point
SEPARATE LIES FROM TRUTH.

This girl was not an at-risk child. She had braces, wore stylish jeans, and cute tennis shoes. The classroom teacher, who heard the whole discussion, said that the girl's parents would be devastated to hear their daughter's misconceptions about sex and dating. During my conversation with the girl, she told me that her "knowledge" of dating had come from teen magazines, the TV shows, and her older sister's friends. Although her parents had done many things right, they were unaware of the lies that swirled in the school halls every day.

We cannot assume our children, whatever ages they may be, will consistently be able to decode the lies from the truth, for lies are packaged so enticingly. We must be informed and bold in pointing out and debunking the lies that can so easily ensnare our children.

key point
STAY INFORMED!

ENCOURAGE YOUR TEEN TO THINK FOR HERSELF AND NOT FALL BACK ON THE "EVERYONE ELSE..." EXCUSE.

TRY THIS!

Help hone your teen's power of discernment. Try saying "That's not true" whenever you hear the following:

- *Everyone else is doing it.*
- *Condoms prevent all STDs.*
- *It's good to be on "the pill just in case.*
- *It's okay if you are in love.*
- *It's okay if you don't go all the way.*
- *Casual sex can have no consequences.*
- *Make it special—save your virginity for prom night.*

DEVELOPMENTAL STAGES

PreTEENS

5th–7th grades or ages 10–12

- Onset of puberty and secondary gender characteristics

- Beginning of self-consciousness about body image; possible eating disorders

- Concrete thinkers

- Primary relationships are still family members, particularly the adults raising them.

- Value same-gender friendships

- Experience homesickness

- Higher need for clear, fair, and consistent boundaries and rules

- Simple and concrete spirituality

- Trying to fit what they've been taught into a concrete worldview

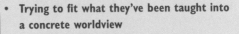

'TWEENagers

6th–9th grades or ages 12–14

- Wide range of physical, emotional, spiritual, intellectual, and social developmental changes and stages

- Mood swings
- Physical and social awkwardness
- Gender differences in social attitudes and behaviors
- Beginnings of abstract thinking
- Difficulty projecting themselves into the future
- Able to understand that behavior has consequences but may not believe the consequences could happen to them.
- Development in sexuality
- Very influenced by peers
- Parents and other adults a major influence
- Importance of same-gender role models
- Continued concrete spiritual questioning

Provide gender-specific information.

Of course men and women are equal, but equal does not mean *identical*. Parents must prepare boys and girls for very different challenges.

Boys need special lessons on respecting women.

You can easily spot the homes in which the father privately shows disrespect for his wife—just watch that dad's little boy. Some men act as though they are "king of their universe," and women exist only to provide them service. But how can a man be a king unless he treats his wife like a queen?

PARENTS POINTER

Having unsupervised cable TV or Internet access in a young boy's room is like putting a bowl of candy bars in the room of a child who is deathly allergic to chocolate. It's a needless and dangerous temptation.

One of the greatest dangers threatening the hearts of our young boys today is the prevalence of pornography. Lust, pornography, and masturbation have reached epidemic proportions within the ranks of Christian men, and it starts at an early age. Pull aside almost any man you know and tell him you are aware that he is struggling with lust. Chances are he will ask, "How did you know?"

How can a man be a king unless he treats his wife like a queen?

Consider the nine-year-old boy who found a *Playboy* magazine in his dad's drawer or the brothers who found a box of porn in the woods behind their fence. They began a dangerous, addictive journey when pornography was introduced into their lives. In time they'll begin to hate themselves and to think there is something wrong with them. We have to help our boys. They can't fight this battle alone.

key point
RESPECTING OTHERS RESPECTS GOD.

key point
BOYS MODEL THEIR DADS.

Talk to your young son about pornography. Be honest about all men having to deal with a battle for their eyes and hearts. You might use the excellent series "Every Man's Battle" to illustrate that no one is alone in these temptations. But after those talks, put all TVs and computers in supervised common rooms. Install a V-Chip in the TV and CYBERsitter (or similar software) on the computer. It's all about respect: respecting women, respecting God, and respecting our boys enough to demand right behavior. Do whatever it takes to win this war. Our young men's hearts are at stake.

TARGET MOMENT

Don't excuse bad behavior by saying, "Boys will be boys." Encourage right and respectful behavior by expecting your son to behave like a young man of God.

Boys need special lessons on growing to be spiritual leaders.

Who was the greatest TV dad of all time? A recent TV Land survey named the two most-admired TV dads of all time: Cliff Huxtable (Bill Cosby) and Andy Griffith, who were tough yet caring, fun-loving, and responsible. Of course, it's a little harder for real dads without a script and dress rehearsals, but every dad longs to personify confident poise and unflappable wisdom.

With Christ as our perfect role model, male leadership is the cornerstone of God's plan for Christian families.

key point
BOYS NEED TO BE TAUGHT TO BE LEADERS.

THE TWO MOST ADMIRED TV DADS OF ALL TIME?

#1: Andy Griffith
(*The Andy Griffith Show*)

#2: Cliff Huxtable
(*The Cosby Show*)

TRY THIS!

Ask your son to name some great biblical leaders and tell what qualities made them great. Point out that Solomon began developing wisdom in childhood, and Paul studied Scripture as a little boy. Jesus showed compassion even during his school years. Let your son know that now is the perfect time to begin to follow in the footsteps of the great men of God.

If men dream of emulating TV dads of heroic proportion, who are our son's heroes? It might surprise you who ranks at the top of that list. It's you, Dad. More boys list their own fathers as their greatest heroes than anyone else in the world. Your son will likely grow up to lead his family in much the same way you are leading yours. Does that comfort or disturb you?

Though all fathers long to be admired and respected, we also are uncomfortably aware of our own embarrassing failings. The real role model is Jesus Christ. Imagine families led by fathers who "do nothing out of selfish ambition or vain conceit, but in humility consider others better than [themselves]" (Philippians 2:3, 4).

BIG BIBLE POINT

Men filled with the love of Christ will raise kids without exasperating them and will not be hard to follow. Read Ephesians 5:25 and 6:4, then ask yourself the following:

- *What examples am I giving my son about living as Christ desires?*
- *What values can I impart to my son to guide him in learning to be a spiritual leader?*
- *Is my son following me in the same ways that I am following Christ?*

Great leaders are not afraid to make difficult decisions or embarrassed to have a heart. Help your son strive for both!

The more closely a man follows the example of Christ, the more he is comfortable being imitated by his own son. Dad is the teacher. Christ is the standard. Much of what a boy needs to learn about sex is really about being disciplined, selfless, patient, and kind. God assigned men as leaders, and Christ shows us that leadership is all about love.

Girls need special lessons on modesty issues.

At what age do we focus on dressing our girls more modestly? Is it when they are "older"? It will probably be too late by then. We are not saying you should dress your little girls like Victorian dolls, but if they wear "hottie" stamped across their backs when they are nine with your blessing, how do you tell them that it's not a great idea when they are sixteen? By the way, it is not a great idea at nine either.

DRESSING MODESTLY CAN BE FUN—AND STYLISH, TOO!

Yes, shopping is hard. Yes, the fashion industry wants our seven-year-old girls to look sixteen and our sixteen-year-olds to look twenty-four. Have you ever considered taking Dad with you when you shop for school clothes or a swimsuit? Does Dad have to be relegated to a fashion show at home after things are purchased or have items hidden from him because he might not approve? He was a teenage boy once, you know. He might have great wisdom on the problem of defining appropriate. Dads, if you are embarrassed by what you daughter wears—or doesn't wear—speak up! We send strong messages about ourselves through our choices of clothing. What message is your daughter sending?

WHEN DECIDING WHAT TO WEAR, REMEMBER: YOUR CLOTHES MAKE A STATEMENT. WHAT DO YOU WANT THEM TO SAY?

Consider the power of having an older high-school or college-age guy speak to your daughters about the effects their choices of clothing have on the opposite sex. When he says that the way some girls dress is like poison to guys and that it makes it hard to respect them as people when they expose a lot of skin, they will listen even more.

Hey, Mom, what do you wear? If you promote your "best assets" to be admired by men other than your husband, don't be surprised when your daughter does the same!

It is very possible to look cool and completely fashionable without sacrificing self-worth. Just ask your daughters this: "Tonight, somewhere, your future husband may be getting ready to go out on a date. You don't know him yet, and he doesn't know you, but someday he will become your soul mate. What do you want *that* girl to wear on her date tonight with *your* future husband?"

key point
CLOTHES MAKE A STATEMENT.

DON'T FORGET

Don't forget that you are the parent. If you don't like the shirt, skirt, shorts, or swimsuit, don't buy it! Period. If it "appears" in your house, make it disappear.

Girls need special lessons on self-esteem.

What happens to our daughters between the ages of eleven and fifteen? Reality hits. They wake up one morning, look around, and realize that there are other girls who are prettier or smarter or richer or more popular, and they often feel that they are at the bottom of the social heap. Even girls who are truly physically attractive will ache for more and feel as if they're less.

key point
BE SUPPORTIVE, FORGIVING— AND LOVING.

key point
BE PATIENT WITH MOOD SWINGS.

This is the time for parents to gently but persistently sustain their daughters through this difficult stage. Please do not view this as a "passing phase"—many adult women still reel from scarred egos arising during those tumultuous middle-school years. The evolving female 'tweenager is a creature who requires much attention, patience, and prayer. As she seems to repel you with her looks and sighs, she is also desperately reaching out to you for comfort and guidance.

"I SPENT THE FIRST FOURTEEN YEARS OF MY LIFE CONVINCED THAT MY LOOKS WERE HIDEOUS. ADOLESCENCE IS PAINFUL FOR EVERYONE."
—Uma Thurman (actress)

It is up to you and other caring adults to help your daughter see her own worth. This assignment is not going to be easy, but it will be worth it!

Moms, don't let yourself forget how hard it was to find your place in the social structure during those 'tween years. And Dads, stand clear of your daughter's raging mood swings, yet stand close enough to hold her when you can. Decide that you are going to calmly deal with the tone in her voice and the way she rolls her eyes that make you wonder what happened to your little girl. She is still your little girl, and she is struggling to find a place where the right boys notice her, the right girls are her friends, and the right clothes are in her closet.

TARGET MOMENT

Engage your blossoming daughter in real-life experiences with you.

- **Help in a community project.**
- **Take a road trip with just one parent.**
- **Let her redecorate her room her way.**
- **Learn a new craft, dance, or sport together.**
- **Approve a new haircut or style.**
- **Find ways to let her shine and feel mature.**

Smooth her path by easing her through the potentially awkward social situations at school and church. Make time for her in your day. Send notes, go to her school events, plan a sleep-over at your place. Tell her you love her and why you are proud of her. She may not acknowledge your extra efforts, but she will appreciate them.

Time for The Talk

Here it is! It's time for The Talk. Yes, you've been dreading it. But the signs are right, your child is seven to nine (or has just passed those ages), and you're running out of excuses. So let's go!

Getting off the ground: How to get started.

All your life you've said you wanted to try skydiving, and today's the day. But now, a thousand feet in the air, you question your sanity. Hey, you've taken the classes. You know you're ready. Go ahead and do it!

Final preparations for The Talk.

Airplane pilots know the value of their final runway check. What if we used that process with our kids? "Potty trained? Check. Going to church? Check. Talked about sex? *Talked about sex?* It's not that big of a deal." Guess what? It *is* that big of a deal. Attention to detail is no more important for the airplanes we ride than for the kids we raise.

So you're finally convinced that your child is ready for The Talk. But you're not so sure about yourself. You knew you would be nervous, but give yourself a little credit. Know it or not, you've already started the process. Have your kids ever seen you kiss or say "I love you" to your spouse? If so, then you've already begun sex education.

THE TALK ISN'T THE FIRST STEP; IT'S JUST THE NEXT STEP.

THERE'S NO TIME LIKE THE PRESENT TO BE-GIN EDUCATING YOUR CHILD. TRUST GOD AND YOURSELF, THEN ... GERONIMO!

key point
THE GOAL IS TO PREPARE OUR KIDS FOR LIFE.

key point
BE BRAVE; YOU CAN DO IT!

In the next few pages is a virtual script that you can literally read aloud to your kids (though your own words would be better). Once you get off the ground you'll be surprised to find that it's easier than you had imagined. Don't chicken out now.

This *really* is it. The day has arrived. You're read-up, pumped-up, and prayed-up. Our goal as parents is to be prepared for The Talk. And the goal of The Talk is that our children be prepared for life. Look around you. The wind is blowing in your face. Go ahead—do it. *Geronimo!*

Review what your kids already know.

You walk into a restaurant with Junior at your side. The look on his face shows he feels important and grown up. What do you say first? Consider: *"Do you know what we're going to talk about today?"* Your child may or may not have guessed the topic of the day. That's okay. You are off the ground. You've begun.

key point
ALLOW ANY QUESTIONS TO BE ASKED.

key point
RELAX AND BE OPEN.

"Today we're going to talk about sex. A lot of kids your age aren't mature enough to understand this subject yet, so I'm going to ask you not to tell very many of your friends about what we discuss."* Her interest is piqued. *"So, what do most of your friends say about sex?"* It works better to ask your child what her friends are saying rather than what she knows. It's much less embarrassing and more likely to reveal useful information. You may find out that your child has been talking about sex quite a bit. You may discover that she barely understands the word.

SHARE YOURSELF!
What is one of the silliest things you've ever believed? Tell your kids about some of the outrageous things you've believed. They'll love it—and it's always healthy to laugh a little at yourself!

"**S**ome kids talk about sex a lot but don't know much about it. Some kids tell each other things that they think are true even though they're not. I remember a time when I thought...." Here's a great place to insert a story about a mistaken belief you had in childhood even if it had nothing to do with sex.

"**Y**ou might have heard and seen things on TV about sex and relationships that aren't true. I really want you to know the truth about sex. Sex is something awesome and wonderful and beautiful that God designed for a husband and wife. I'm excited that we're talking about it. Today I want to answer any questions you have. No question is off limits. Ask anything you want." Your child may have questions right off the bat ... or she may sit silently. She may shuffle her feet under the table. She may stare at you wide-eyed or not look at you at all. But she will listen (carefully), and she will hang on every word. We're flying now. Time to bring it all home.

> **ESPECIALLY IN TALKING WITH YOUR 'TWEEN, IT'S HELPFUL TO:**
>
> • Maintain a nonjudgmental attitude.
>
> • Encourage your child to ask questions.
>
> • Keep your sense of humor, calm, and patience.
>
> • Use words that are understandable.
>
> • Relate sex to love, intimacy, caring, and respect.
>
> • Be open in sharing your values and concerns.

Bring the message home: God made sex for marriage.

This is the hardest part. There is a time to be particularly frank, honest, and clear. And that time is now.

Explain the "plumbing" and be honest about sex.

What is the right way to tell your child that sex involves a penis going into a vagina? You may have heard funny stories about parents telling stories about trains going into tunnels. Really, there is no perfectly comfortable way to share this information. Be prepared to feel a little embarrassed, but don't shy away from the truth. Sending a hazy message at this point can leave room for misunderstandings.

Remember why you are doing this. You have decided to courageously put aside your own discomfort and share the truth before you have to unteach misinformation. Be proud of yourself. This is your job, and you're doing it. Nobody said it would be easy—just that it would be worth it.

key point
NOBODY SAID THIS WOULD BE EASY.

WHEN THE BIG MOMENT ARRIVES ...
- Be prepared to feel a little embarrassed.
- Don't shy away from the truth.
- Use correct terminology.
- Be detailed. Be clear. Be accurate.
- Avoid mysterious or ambiguous language.

"*When two people are married, they love each other in a very special way. They hug and kiss each other differently. Because they are married, a husband and wife can sometimes be together without clothes on and not be embarrassed, like Adam and Eve in the Garden of Eden. During sex they hug and kiss with no clothes, and the husband fits his penis into the wife's vagina. Something called sperm goes from the husband into the wife, and they both feel close and happy, and their bodies feel good all over. The sperm is what plants a tiny baby in the mother. Neither parent can make a child alone, but together sex can begin the life of a new baby.*"

Remember why you are having The Talk:

- **Your kids will learn about sex somewhere from someone.**
- **Poorly Informed friends will pass on misconceptions.**
- **Irresponsible media passes on lies and half-truths.**
- **You don't want to have to unteach misinformation.**
- **You're the perfect person to teach your child the truth!**

key point

YOUR TIME AND LOVE WILL BE WORTH IT!

"Ewwww! Gross!" Not an improbable response from a child learning the plumbing of sex for the first time.

Don't let such reactions bother you. They are really just healthy expressions of that natural sense of modesty you've helped your child develop. Don't go overboard with information. Focus on basic biological science. For today, concentrate on the mechanics of how a baby is created. It's beautiful, it's natural, and it's God's idea.

Set the bar high for love and marriage.

"*I know sex may sound gross at first. I felt like that when I was your age. But a few years from now you won't feel that way. Actually, sex is God's idea, and He intended it to be a beautiful part of the love between a husband and wife. Sex is part of God's way to make sure that every baby has both a mom and a dad. God wants love to be the foundation of every family.*"

key point
SET HIGH STANDARDS FOR SEX, LOVE, AND MARRIAGE.

This would be an excellent time to tell your child a few details surrounding the story of her own birth: how you dreamed about your new baby, how you chose her name, and other fun facts during the days before her birth. The point is to plant an initial understanding of the fact that sex is something planned by God for married couples who love each other. There is no need to provide all details of your courtship, but remind your child that God wants kids to be born of love into loving families.

"A successful marriage requires falling in love many times, always with the same person."
—Mignon McLaughlin

TRY THIS!

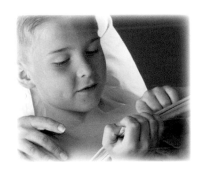

Share your child's baby album and take a walk down memory lane. You may wish to let your child help organize any loose pictures into a fresh, new album he can keep and look through as he chooses!

Kids love to hear the story of their own births! Share some of the following with your child:

• Did I move a lot while I was in your tummy?

• What time was I born? How big was I?

• Were we in a hospital? How long did we stay?

• Who was the first one to hold me?

• Did I have hair? Did I smile?

Your child may ask an awkward question: "Do you and Daddy ever do that ... sex thing?" A simple yes should suffice with an explanation of how blessed you are to have been given such an awesome child as God's gift. She may add, "How often do people do it? Can I watch?" This is the time to be calm, cool, and not overreactive; answer simply and honestly.

Remember that your purpose at this point in The Talk is to set high standards for sex, love, and marriage. Don't waver. You are painting a beautiful picture of what a godly, loving home looks like. Your child will carry this picture with her, and its simple beauty will enable her to avoid many of the tempting shortcuts and dangerous pitfalls she will encounter. You know what you want for your child: godly choices, a clear conscience, a great marriage, and wonderful kids of her own!

key point
BE CLEAR, CONFIDENT, AND COURAGEOUS.

Having sex has consequences.

*"You're gonna reap what you sow.
You're gonna eat what your garden grows.
Don't be deceived. Please believe.
You're gonna reap what you sow."*
(from "The Reaping Rap," by Ron Duer)

There are good consequences when sex is right.

Our Savior used tiny mustard seeds to illustrate the growing power of faith. Less-desirable seeds that also experience growth include weeds and thorns. Although both look similar, remember that what we plant matters. The sexual decisions of your kids are "mustard-seed" decisions. They may start small, but before long their impact and consequences are enormous.

"Jesus grew in wisdom and stature, and in favor with God and man" (Luke 2:52). This verse describes the growth of the Son of God in each major developmental category: spiritual, physical, intellectual, emotional, and social. (Use the acronym SPIES to remember the list.) These categories also outline positive and negative consequences of sexual involvement. There *are* good and bad consequences from decisions about sexual behavior. Try this activity to illustrate those consequences with your child.

It does matter what we plant, for we reap what we sow!

Get several packets of seeds, including fruits, vegetables, or flowers. Mix the seeds. (Make sure you know the difference.) Tell your kids you've brought seeds for two different plants (such as strawberries and eggplant). Ask your child if it matters which seeds are planted and why. Now make the application: *You reap what you sow.*

You teach your children daily about love and respect as they watch how you treat the people whom you love.

God made sex to be a special expression of love between a husband and a wife. When they have sex only with each other, they feel wonderful and close. Sex God's way is like planting seeds of love. The husband and wife respect each other. They enjoy being together. They are proud of what God is growing in their lives.

TIPS FOR 'TWEENS

Remind your 'tween that sexual choices and behaviors affect us in a number of ways (SPIES).

Socially: friends, family, and romance

Physically: pregnancy and STDs

Intellectually: educational decisions

Emotionally: self-esteem and other issues of the heart

Spiritually: closeness and obedience to God

key point
YOU REAP WHAT YOU SOW.

key point
SEXUAL CHOICES HAVE CONSEQUENCES.

There are bad consequences when sex is wrong.

You have just painted a beautiful picture of the wonderful consequences of sexuality God's way. Your child may or may not be impressed, but he *is* catching on to the idea that sex is something God planned for married couples. Your child knows that sex makes babies and that God wants those babies to be born into loving, caring families. You have planted the concepts of love, fidelity, loyalty, and respect. It's time to finish the message: *Not everyone listens to God. Some people make wrong decisions, and those decisions have consequences, too.*

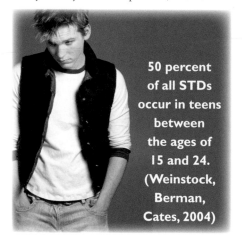

50 percent of all STDs occur in teens between the ages of 15 and 24. (Weinstock, Berman, Cates, 2004)

key point
SEXUAL DISEASES DO HAPPEN!

Your child needs to understand that sin always hurts people. God's doesn't want anyone to get hurt, so He's told us to save sex until marriage. Having sex when you are not married is like putting your hand on a red-hot stove—you only end up getting burned.

Our most requested presentation, and the one that seems to get the strongest reaction, covers sexually transmitted diseases, or STDs. Now, of course you know The Talk is not the time to go into detail on the symptoms of genital herpes or the rate of cervical cancer, but your child does need to know about sexually transmitted diseases.

STDs: **The Big Six**
Estimated numbers of new cases annually

Genital Warts Human Papillomavirus [HPV]: 6,200,000
50% of sexually active people test positive.

Chlamydia: 3,000,000
1 in 10 sexually active adolescent females test positive.

Herpes: 1,000,000
1 in 5 over the age of 11 test positive.

Gonorrhea: 650,000
75% of infections occur in 15- to 29-year-olds.

Syphilis: 70,000

HIV: 40,000

(Centers for Disease Control, 2003)

Today dozens of STDs exist, most notably the "big six," including genital herpes, chlamydia, genital warts, and AIDS. Genital warts alone infect half of sexually active Americans. It's okay to briefly explain to your child the damage wrong sex can do to people's hearts, relationships, reputations, and spirits. Be real. Be honest. But don't stay negative for long. They'll get the point pretty quickly!

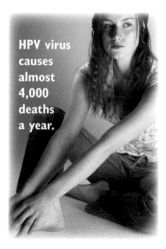

HPV virus causes almost 4,000 deaths a year.

Use Teachable Moments

By now you have caught on to the fact that talking to your kids about sex is an ongoing process. With that in mind, let's explore some time-honored methods of bringing up the subject while making it all appear ever so casual.

Use media moments.

We live in a media-saturated society where media images create lasting impressions—both positive and negative. Many of those images can be used to create unrepeatable, teachable moments with our children.

Discuss positive messages and images.

Last Valentine's Day a news segment on TV interviewed couples who had recently celebrated their golden anniversaries and shared their personal "secrets of success." Couples touted the virtues of communication, humor, and commitment. With so many things wrong in our world it's great to occasionally pause and consider the things going right.

key point

SHINE A SPOTLIGHT ON WHAT'S GOING RIGHT.

Christian books, videos, movies, and especially music with direct Christian messages are more available, of higher quality, and are experiencing greater widespread acceptance than ever. If you don't know much about contemporary Christian music and books, take a brief tour of your local Christian bookstore. You may be surprised by what you discover.

Media doesn't have to be distinctly Christian to be positive. The TV show portraying a loving family, the movie about a man who sticks with his wife through a battle with cancer, the song about a husband and wife expecting their first child—each of these images presents an opportunity to capture a teachable moment about families and relationships.

Consider this: How well do we model appropriate entertainment viewing? If it's not okay for our 'tweens to watch, is it really the best show for us to watch?

TURN OFF THE TUBE AND TUNE IN TO YOUR KIDS!

Each year, most children in the United States spend about 1,500 hours in front of the television, compared with 900 hours in school and only 33 hours in meaningful conversation with their parents!

Even plot lines involving imperfect characters leading imperfect lives can provide teachable moments, if the shows are honest. We are not talking about a growing list of sexually charged teen comedies where irresponsible sexual choices and images drive the first nine-tenths of the movie. Such shows are exploitative and dangerous. We'll talk more about those programs next.

Discuss negative messages and images.

No matter how much we try to guard against and guide responses to the negative influences exerted on our kids, we cannot control them all. We can't put our children in barrels or lock them in attics. What can we do? With a little creativity, we can use even the most negative media influences as conversation starters for discussing how God wants us to deal with controversial issues.

What would you think of your 'tween watching a movie about a sixteen-year-old girl who thinks she is truly in love with a guy she has never spoken to and whom her father has forbidden her to see? The movie just described is *The Little Mermaid*. Now, we don't hate this movie; in fact, we own it. But we realize there can be dangers in shows that have traditionally been considered "safe."

key point

LOVE IS A DECISION— NOT JUST A FEELING.

Go to GetNetWise.com or safekids.com for information and filtering software to help block children's exposure to inappropriate Internet materials.

Many programs contain underlying messages that, if not discussed, can be very harmful to our children. We sometimes overlook the media's faulty definition of love. How are we teaching our children to handle the feelings that come with that first crush and the overwhelming swell of emotions? Unfortunately, media rarely teaches our children the difference between real, sacrificial, life-long, committed love and infatuation.

TARGET MOMENT

Help your kids separate reality from fiction. For example, when your child watches *Cinderella*, help her realize it is a nice but made-up story by saying, "You know, this isn't real; they didn't even know each other" or "That should have been their first date, not the day they decided to get married."

Help your kids fight the social pressures of what "everyone" is watching and find suitable alternatives. Remind them when something is fantasy and not real. Our children will be in situations where they will have to decide by themselves what movies to watch or magazines to read or music to hear. We can't always be there—but our influence and wisdom can offer guidance for a lifetime!

Check this out!

25% OF KIDS 2–5 HAVE A TV IN THEIR BEDROOMS.

52% OF KIDS 5–17 HAVE A TV IN THEIR BEDROOMS.

54% OF KIDS 4–6 CHOOSE TV OVER SPENDING TIME WITH THEIR DADS.

(Center for Media Education and the A. C. Nielsen Company)

Use illustrations and object lessons.

If you want to teach your kids about sex, imitate the Master Teacher by using stories, illustrations, and object lessons whenever you can.

Use stories with a message.

Here are three stories we believe will take powerful, positive messages about sex and "burn them" into the memory banks of your children. Just as the story of Moses and the Red Sea will forever symbolize God's protection for His people, these stories will convey fundamental truths about the beauty, weightiness, and incredible value of God's plan for sex.

"**T**he Gold Locket," by Robert Wolgemuth (ages 9–12): This short story begins with a young man's first crush on a young woman. As Christmas approaches, he looks for a present that will express his affection for her. He finally settles on a beautiful golden locket. "The Gold Locket" perfectly illustrates how premarital sex dilutes and trivializes the commitments made in marriage.

key point
IMITATE THE MASTER TEACHER—JESUS.

key point
USE STORIES, ILLUSTRATIONS, AND OBJECT LESSONS.

"The Marriage Roses," by Marvin Payne (ages 5–12): Here is a fairy tale in a land where each marriage is begun by planting a magical rose bush. Sadly, a day comes when sickness spreads across the land. Could the culprit be a salesman who peddles fake marriage roses that are less expensive and easy to grow? "The Marriage Roses" provides an honest look at the hurt that occurs when wedding vows are cheapened or ignored.

BIG BIBLE POINT

What is love? Read aloud with your child I Corinthians 13:1-8, 13. Then guide your child to understand that love is deep, abiding, and pure.

- *What qualities does love have?*
- *How is love different from infatuation or a "crush?*
- *In what ways does love involve our spiritual, physical, and emotional selves?*
- *Is just saying the words "I love you" proof of love? Explain.*

You Are Special, by Max Lucado (ages 3–12): In the land of small puppet people called Wemmicks, a puppet struggles to believe in himself and discovers a secret that changes his life forever. *You Are Special* packs a surprising spiritual punch. The solution to battling low self-esteem lies neither in maximizing personal positives nor in minimizing individual shortcomings but in knowing how deeply you are cherished by the Maker.

TRY THIS!

William Bennett's The Book of Virtues **is an excellent resource for meaningful stories and illustrations on themes such as self-discipline, responsibility, honesty, loyalty, and faith. Many applications to sexuality are both obvious and powerful.**

Use object talks with a message.

Jesus was not only a master storyteller. He also frequently used object lessons—simple, everyday illustrations that enlightened His powerful messages. *"Consider the lilies of the field." "Faith is like a mustard seed."* Look around you for visual aids that make your lessons on sex understandable and memorable. Here are three of our favorite object lessons.

key point
VISUAL AIDS MAKE LESSONS MEMORABLE.

PARENTS POINTER

Tell kids pornography is like a "chocolate-covered roach":

- **The appearance makes you want to try it.**
- **It fools you into thinking it might be enjoyable.**
- **The attraction is a paper-thin veneer.**
- **After you try it, you realize it's disgusting.**
- **The next time, it may be tempting all over again.**
- **You are much better off never to have tasted it.**

Bonded for Life (ages 7–12+): Cut four long strips of packing tape. The pieces of tape represent people and that God intends for sex to glue people to each other (Matthew 19:5). Stick two pieces together with the sticky sides, then try to separate them. Take the other two pieces and press and peel them on and off your arms several times. Now try to bond those two pieces to each other. The application is powerful: Multiple sex partners reduce the ability to bond with a life-long mate (adapted from *Choosing the Best* curriculum).

The Heat Is On (ages 10–12+): While working in the kitchen, ask the kids if they know how to cook a frog. The idea is gross enough to spike their interest. Tell them that cold-blooded animals like frogs cannot feel temperature around them changing, since their body temperatures merely match that of their environment. Inform your kids that if they put a frog in a pot and raise the heat slowly enough, they can cook a frog to death, and it will never try to escape—it won't even notice the danger until it's too late. The application is simple. There are sexual activities that most people believe they would never consider. But after slowly turning up the sexual heat, little by little, unsuspecting people can find themselves in dangerous waters, about to get deeply hurt.

Dangerous Tastes (ages 10–12+): Put a half-teaspoon of salt into one cup and sugar into another. Confuse the cups until you have no idea which contains what without tasting. Then select a cup and shake the contents into your mouth. Let your child know that it is equally difficult to tell whether or not a person has a sexually transmitted disease. People with and without diseases often look the same on the outside.

THE NEWS IS GOOD:
According to the Centers for Disease Control, the percentage of sexually active preteens and teens has decreased over the past ten years, as have certain risky sexual behaviors.

Use or defuse sex-ed programs in your child's school.

Controversy concerning school-taught sex education has gained new fuel over the last ten years. If you pay school taxes, you are a consumer of that school's product, and you need to know what you are getting for your dollar!

Know what is being taught at school.

Bet you're thinking, "Good, this is a chapter I won't have to read for a while. My child is not even in fourth grade yet." Well, have a seat and get comfortable. There is a growing trend of teaching human sexuality within the younger grades—sometimes even in kindergarten. So, what can you expect? At the least, your child will be shown a "gender-specific video" sometime between the fourth and sixth grades. At the most, your child could be taught many "facts" that may not be in agreement with your family values.

key point
KNOW WHAT VALUES YOUR CHILD IS BEING TAUGHT.

If your child is in fourth grade, ask the teacher when the sessions on human sexuality are scheduled to be taught. If the program does not use videos, they may not send home a permission slip, and you will have no idea when and what is being presented to your child at school.

A program is unsuitable for sixth grade if:

- Alternative lifestyles are discussed as normal.
- Detailed pictures of human anatomy are shown in coed classes.
- Condoms are promoted as a viable option to prevent pregnancy or disease.
- Parents are not informed, not allowed to preview, or not allowed to pull their child from the course.

There are some gender-specific videos of tolerable quality that stick to the basics of anatomy, puberty, and maturation. These are usually viewed with boys and girls separated and, it is hoped, preceded by a notification slip requesting parental permission for the viewing. Our suggestion is that you ask to view the video and any handouts before the class showing.

Many schools that use maturation videos are becoming aware that children need much more training on the subjects of boundaries, modesty, appropriate behavior, unwanted pregnancy, and disease—yes, in sixth

grade. Do not pull your child from a program that seems too advanced until you have talked with teachers and other parents about what is being discussed at recess, on the bus, and at sleep-overs.

EVEN SIXTH-GRADERS ARE FREQUENTLY EXPOSED TO CONVERSATIONS AND JOKES WITH SEXUAL INNUENDOES.

After you have viewed the videos and the handouts, it would be wise to discuss with your child what will be shown at school. You can plan ahead for two great opportunities for teachable moments: preparing your child for viewing the video, then following up with a how-did-it-go discussion.

Decide if the school's teaching contradicts your values.

If you are not pleased with the information the school plans to teach, take steps to make those concerns heard. You could choose not to sign the permission slip, and your little Johnny or Johnette will spend an hour in the library while the rest of the class views the video. In that case, you will need to discuss your decision with your child so he or she can be armed to handle questioning peers.

key point

THE VOICE OF REASON IS MOST READILY HEARD.

Even if your child does not participate, he will hear everything that was taught—and peers will be the teachers. You must remember that most of your child's peers will not receive any instruction at home and will be the source of inaccuracies. It is your job to teach your child and to have a positive effect on your child's environment.

"BEFORE THE CHILD EVER GETS TO SCHOOL HE WILL HAVE RECEIVED CRUCIAL, ALMOST IRREVOCABLE SEX EDUCATION AND THIS WILL HAVE BEEN TAUGHT BY THE PARENTS, WHO ARE NOT AWARE OF WHAT THEY ARE DOING."

—DR. MARY S. CALDERONE

Many schools form an advisory board consisting of teachers and parents to help with curriculum selection. If you discover that your child is being taught human sexual anatomy and behavior without your consent, then action is warranted. But righteous indignation will get you little except a reputation as a troublemaker. And please, do not assume that your school administrators are "evil incarnate."

key point
ASK FOR GOD'S GUIDANCE THROUGH PRAYER.

While showing respect for their positions, approach the administrators with calm determinedness. State your concerns, offer alternatives, and bring letters of support if needed. Investigate the sex-education programs of other schools and check the More Resources list at the end of this book. Calmly and prayerfully remember that most administrators like kids and want the best for them. Use your passion on this topic, but also use your head, your skills of persuasion, and your discernment as you ask the school to reconsider their programming.

MAKE SURE THE SCHOOL RECOGNIZES YOU AS THE VOICE OF REASON AND CONCERN— NOT AS A FANATICAL NAYSAYER TRYING TO RIOT THE MASSES.

TARGET MOMENT
What if I don't let my child watch "the video"? Will this mar him for life? Probably not. Would my child be marred if he stayed in the class and watched the questionable video? Probably not.

Use your personal stories.

Everyone has a story to tell, and your kids will love to hear yours. If you have the courage, both your successes and disappointments can be powerful learning opportunities for your kids!

Share your successes.

Success breeds success, so it stands to reason that we should share our victories with our children to encourage and empower them to make their own positive decisions. Don't shy away from letting your children know about the blessings that come when dating, love, and sex are done in the right way.

TARGET MOMENT

A loving, intimate relationship between two parents strengthens our children's sexual health and integrity ... and helps them make good choices when it's time!

TRY THIS!

Our daughters love the story of our first kiss. We had been dating for five weeks and never kissed. One evening we stopped to sit and talk. Clumsily, I leaned toward Shannon and asked as romantically as I could, "May I kiss you?" Imagine my surprise when she replied, "Come over here and get it!" The kids enjoy teasing us both about that story.

Make a scrapbook of your dating memories to share with your kids as they enter the dating phase in a few years. Add pictures and short paragraphs about times, people, and places you remember—and what you learned from them!

key point
SHARE YOURSELF WITH YOUR KIDS.

Even that college-days anecdote has several underlying messages we're glad to share with our kids. We communicated intentionally (although clumsily) about our physical and emotional relationship. Such transparency on our part makes our kids much more likely to share some of their own emotional and relational ups and downs with us.

You don't have to have been perfect to have inspirational stories to tell your kids about things you did right. Did you ever say something to a boyfriend that you later regretted? Did you learn anything during your dating years about honesty, trust, or respect? Did anything in your dating life reflect the fruit of the Spirit's influence, such as love, joy, peace, patience, kindness, goodness, faithfulness, gentleness, and self-control? (Share Galatians 5:22, 23 with your kids!) If so, you've got stories to tell. Even silly, seemingly neutral anecdotes about your dating days will teach your children volumes about what is normal and healthy. Tell your stories to your kids—it's a gift no one else can give them.

key point
KIDS LEARN FROM YOUR EXAMPLES!

"A loving family provides the foundation children need to succeed, and strong families with a man and a woman—bonded together for life—always have been, and always will be, the key to such families."
—Jim Bunning

Share your disappointments.

How can we use disappointments as teachable moments when we would rather forget about them? Although we never want to go through life's hard times, they do give us unique insights into the plight of fellow travelers as they fall into the same potholes and cry out for help.

TARGET MOMENT

How can we use our disappointments as teachable moments when we would rather forget about them? One hopes we remember what caused the mistakes and how we avoided them next time. Couldn't your child use some of that insight?

key point

SMART PEOPLE LEARN FROM THEIR MISTAKES.

What does sharing our disappointments and mistakes about dating and relationships entail? It could be a retelling of the time you went out with your best friend's boyfriend while she was out of town or the party you attended that you shouldn't have. There may be stories of the guys you used to make yourself feel popular or the girl you used just so you wouldn't feel lonely. We haven't always been the wise, kind people we are today. Some of us were real jerks. Our tendency toward "jerkdom" explains the low attendance at many high-school and college reunions.

You may be asking, "Why would I want to share these historic tidbits with my children?" Perhaps you don't, or even shouldn't, want to tell your kids about your mistakes—that's your call. But you may realize what good lessons those stories could teach when you are trying to share certain values and concepts. We're not just talking dating stories here—we're talking life stories. How about the time you didn't get invited to the party or the time that you were hurt by a friend's gossip? We didn't all make the team or the grade, and none of us survived school without a few scars. How did that feel? What did you learn? Couldn't your child use some of that insight as well?

key point

REALLY SMART PEOPLE LEARN FROM OTHERS'

Life has brought you here. Share that life—and life's lessons—with your child.

Be prepared! One day your child could innocently ask you, "Did you and Mom wait until you were married?" Decide now what you will say. Be sure you and your spouse are in full agreement on how to answer that question. When your children see you paid the consequences, they can protect themselves. When they see you repented, they can accept God's forgiveness.

A flat-out lie is not the best choice, but you can choose to guard the truth.

A final word ...

A few years ago when our daughters were seven and twelve, I (Karl) was driving along when it dawned on me that this was an opportunity to bring up almost any subject without fear that either girl would bail out of the car. "What do you think are the biggest mistakes parents make when they talk to their kids about sex?" I asked in my best nonchalant voice.

key point
CLOSE
THE
BOOK...

Silence. Deathly silence. No worry. Silence gives time to think. Good leaders tolerate silence to receive quality answers to difficult questions. Finally Katie, our eldest, spoke up. "I think," she began, "the biggest mistake parents make in talking to their kids about sex is that they just never get around to it. A lot of parents just never even bring the subject up." *Wow,* I thought. "Excellent point," I said. In fact, that point is so vital that we have spent the first chapter of this book trying to convince you of the importance of parental involvement in the sexual education of your children.

DON'T FORGET

You already have the love. You know you have the responsibility. You have gained the knowledge. It's not too soon, and it's not too late.

I knew if I could stay quiet I might hear another gem. That intuition paid off. "I think," started Sammy, "that parents talk about it too much, and they make it sound all nasty and dirty." Out of the mouths of babes. How many parents accidentally allow a godly passion for their children's purity to spawn periodic tirades about the dangers and evil of sex.

TARGET MOMENT

1. **Just do it.** Talk to your kids about sex.

2. **Make it positive.** Sex is a beautiful gift from a loving God.

key point
... AND OPEN YOUR HEART!

There you have it. These two simple principles sum up our entire message. Number one: *Just do it.* It's your responsibility. You are your child's best teacher because no one cares as deeply about the outcome as you do. Number two: *Make it positive.* Sex is not a four-letter word. It's a beautiful gift from a loving God. That's it. Seminar over. Closing credits. *Just do it* and *make it positive.*

Remember ... If you don't teach them, someone else will!

More Resources

BOOKS
for kids
- Carol Greene, *Why Boys and Girls Are Different* (Concordia Publishing House, 1998). Ages 3–5.
- Stan and Brenna Jones, *The Story of Me* (NavPress, 1995). Ages 3–5.
- Max Lucado, *You Are Special* (Crossway Books, 1997). Ages 3–12.
- Stan and Brenna Jones, *What's The Big Deal?* (NavPress, 1995). Ages 5–8.
- Carolyn Nystrom, *Before I Was Born* (NavPress, 1995). Ages 5–8.
- Marvin Payne, "The Marriage Roses" (in Linda and Richard Eyre, *How to Talk to Your Child About Sex*, St. Martin's Press, 1998). Ages 5–12.
- Ruth Hummell, *Where Do Babies Come From?* (Concordia Publishing House, 1998). Ages 6–8.
- Jane Graver, *How You Are Changing* (Concordia Publishing House, 1998). Ages 8–11.
- Robert Wolgemuth, "The Gold Locket" (*Campus Life* 57 [November/December 1988]; for reprint information, call 630-260-6200 or e-mail clmag@CampusLife.net). Ages 9–12.

for parents
- Mark Laaser, *Talking to Your Kids About Sex.* (WaterBrook Press, 1999).
- Linda and Richard Eyre, *How to Talk to Your Child About Sex* (St. Martin's Press, 1998).
- Kevin Leman and Kathy Flores Bell, *A Chicken's Guide to Talking Turkey With Your Kids About Sex* (Zondervan, 2004).

WEB SITES

- www.GetNetWise.com. Filtering software for your computer.
- www.safekids.com. Filtering software for your computer.
- www.talkingwithkids.org/sex.html. Kaiser Family Foundation affiliate.
- www.betterhealth. Tips and guides for teaching about tough issues.

Subpoint Index

Chapter 1: If You Don't Teach Them, Someone Else Will   8

We didn't hear it from our parents. 8
We feel too uncomfortable. 10
Media: We're not in Mayberry any more! 12
"But, my best friend said…" 14
The Bible addresses the issue of teaching kids about sex. 16
These "talks" are our responsibility—both Mom's and Dad's. ...18
These are always ongoing chats and talks. 20
These talks should be positive. 22
Give focused attention with time and listening. 24
Realize that everything you do communicates to your child. 26
Make it fun—if you can. 28

Chapter 2: It's Not Too Soon; It's Not Too Late   30

God made your body and said, "It is good!" 30
Boys and girls are different. 32
Privacy, modesty, and respect all matter! 34
God wants kids to be raised by loving families. 36
Little questions deserve little answers. 38
Heighten their curiosity and anticipation. 40
Make your child feel "grown up." 42
Puberty, growth, and change do happen! 44
Be forewarned and forearmed! 46
Don't avoid the tough topics. 48
Debunking the lies. 50

Developmental Stages (ages 10–14 chart). 52
Boys need special lessons on respecting women. 54
Boys need special lessons on growing to be spiritual leaders. ...56
Girls need special lessons on modesty issues. 58
Girls need special lessons on self-esteem. 60

Chapter 3: Time for The Talk   62

Final preparations for The Talk. 62
Review what your kids already know. 64
Explain the "plumbing" and be honest about sex. 66
Set the bar high for love and marriage. 68
There are good consequences when sex is right. 70
There are bad consequences when sex is wrong. 72

Chapter 4: Use Teachable Moments   74

Discuss positive messages and images. 74
Discuss negative messages and images. 76
Use stories with a message. 78
Use object talks with a message. 80
Know what is being taught at school. 82
Decide if the school's teaching contradicts your values. 84
Share your successes. 86
Share your disappointments. 88
A final word. 90